Worry the Dead

poems by

Kelly A. Jones

Finishing Line Press
Georgetown, Kentucky

Worry the Dead

Copyright © 2016 by Kelly A. Jones
ISBN 978-1-63534-046-4 First Edition
All rights reserved under International and Pan-American Copyright Conventions.
No part of this book may be reproduced in any manner whatsoever without written permission from the publisher, except in the case of brief quotations embodied in critical articles and reviews.

ACKNOWLEDGMENTS

For publishing some of these poems in their previous form, grateful acknowledgment is made to:

Buried Letter Press, "Whiskey and an Apology"
Indy Week, "Ruby-throated Goner"
NYSAI Press, "I've Tried to Erase This Image"
The Rain, Party, & Disaster Society, "Fragile Feathered Friends"
Rat's Ass Review, "Good Luck"
Rougarou Literary Journal, "The Gulf Between Us"
Samizdat Literary Journal, "To Save, Press 9"

And lots of love and appreciation goes out to friends and family. Thanks to all who read drafts, gave opinions, provided distractions, and made the world a happier and more fun place to be. ♥

Publisher: Leah Maines

Editor: Christen Kincaid

Cover Art: Ted Morée

Author Photo: Ted Morée

Printed in the USA on acid-free paper.
Order online: www.finishinglinepress.com
also available on amazon.com

Author inquiries and mail orders:
Finishing Line Press
P. O. Box 1626
Georgetown, Kentucky 40324
U. S. A.

Table of Contents

How Much Damage We Could Do 1

I've Tried to Erase This Image 2

Whiskey and an Apology 3

Fragile Feathered Friend 4

Recalled 5

Ruby-throated Goner 7

Going, Going, Gone 8

Good Luck 9

Us Lost Boys 10

I Am Not Afraid 11

More than Zero 12

Carry On, Carrion 13

Under the Sea 14

Día de Muertos, 2015 15

To Save, Press 9 16

The Gulf Between 17

We're Wireless 18

Dedicated to all our ghosts

How Much Damage We Could Do

I was in love with his hair when we were younger.
Nights were spent shooting Jack and smoking Camels.
Recruited at twenty, he sweated through summer
in South Carolina. Basic training sucked away at him.
He swatted mosquitoes at night, bloodied his fingers.
When his sign-on bonus came he bought a tacky sports car,
then sped down highways, just a purple blur against asphalt.
He used to be longhaired and lanky; sported a stoned grin.
We'd bruise each other up while wrestling around at parties.
Friends would watch and place cheap bets on who'd win.

I've Tried to Erase This Image

After Saddam Hussein's execution
my friend's unit was stationed at one of his castles.

In the picture he emailed me: soldiers, Humvees, weapons,
camouflage, potted flowers, and some men barbecuing meat.

Rows of palm trees are off to the sides, like paradise,
like Hollywood, like places tourists flock to.

It almost looked like a bachelor party,
all those suntans and smiles.

Whiskey and an Apology

Two pictures flanked the casket: one, a soldier, the other a Muay Thai fighter. I kept looking for a picture I knew, but that white-trash hippie had been gone for years. His plan had been to play Army, then move to Thailand. He'd asked me to visit him there. That afternoon men in Army uniforms called him a hero as I muttered angrily with our friends. In Thailand, a funeral lasts at least a week. Crying is discouraged. Mourners try not to worry the dead with their suffering. Outside, bikers kept anti-war protestors from disturbing the service. I never cry at funerals. I cry making coffee or watching a movie or looking for button mushrooms at the store. At Thai funerals monks come and go, reciting prayers and preparing the spirit to move forward. When the redneck bikers left, after the casket was lowered and the mourners had gone away, I went to the grave with Jack Daniels and candles. People had already left dog tags and American flags, fake flowers and little crosses. Thai mourners make a book containing the story of the deceased. They write poems about them and leave them on an altar. Here.

Fragile Feathered Friend

Last week on the dunes at Carolina Beach
I found a bird's wing in a clump of sea grass.

I was still living in Seattle when he died,
got home and found a crow on my porch.

When the crow flew at my screen door
I asked what it wanted.

When he enlisted
I told him *it's your funeral.*

When the crow cawed a reply I said *sorry,
I don't understand, there's nothing I can do.*

I took the beached wing home with me, turned the bones
into a wind-chime to hang by my window.

My wind-chime never makes noise
but on gusty days it spins around beautifully.

In Seattle I called a friend to tell them about a bird I saw
flying against a building repeatedly. They told me I was crazy.

That crow stayed on my porch all night
as I sat in the kitchen, drinking him goodbye.

Recalled

Late this summer I received a letter warning me
that the car I drove was defective and its airbag,
if deployed, could shoot shards of metal into my lungs.

It said "deployed," as if a drive is a mission
and highways are combat zones.

I work at a literacy center
and the language I use
is surprisingly militaristic.
I give students batteries of tests.
We drill them on phonemes
and I recruit volunteers for days of service.

For 9/11 I made a sign on poster board
that students and volunteers wrote on.
They shared what they remembered from that day
and why they were thankful for those who have fought
terrorism ever since the towers fell.

I didn't sign it because I couldn't think of anything to say
that could sit for a week on a table
between books about heroes and comics about war.
But I did draw a bird flying between
the two columns of signatures and stories.

I don't have panic attacks anymore but I do say
fuck this a lot. I would be so pissed
if I died in a fender bender
because safety equipment failed me.

It has been seven years since Bird disappeared in the desert
after the unarmored Humvee he was in exploded.

He once told me he was risking his life
because he'd rather die doing something.

It has been fourteen years since the towers came down.
I once thought that under the rubble we'd find a new beginning.

Ruby-throated Goner

One minute those birds were soaring up above, the next they were on the ground. When I was young my best friend lived in a trailer by the lake. He was Bird and I was Bones. I grew up between the cemetery and a tobacco field. We would smoke while walking between the two, thinking not of irony, but destiny. When Bird told me he'd enlisted I said *it's your funeral*. He looked at me through eyes I later described in a poem as hummingbird blue and told me he knew. News varied about what caused the animals to cease flight: electricity, temperature changes, or radio waves. Bird died in a desert because bone fragments punctured his lungs and he drowned there in the sand, in his own body. The mass die-off made more sense to me, reminded me of worms that washed out of the dirt during heavy storms then dried up on the road. The first time I saw this it didn't shock me, just worms being worms and then not being worms. I don't understand war. Bird was a soldier and then an explosion. The last time he kissed me I told him it was too late, that he was gone and I should be going. I stayed and we drank and he curled into my side. In the daylight he pecked me goodbye, or maybe good morning. Now Bird's hollow and covered with dirt. I'm no longer certain if his eyes were blue. He is gone for good, and I just can't remember.

Going, Going, Gone

When I was working at a library
a teen asked me for books about war.
He had brown eyes and he was smiling.
I wanted to recommend some anti-war novels,
but led him to the nonfiction section
where we flipped through indices
for battles and heroes.

He looked like a soldier: shaved head and muscular
arms that reminded me of the boys I grew up with.
Those boys who died in a desert en route
to some shoot out or scouting mission.
Their names are not in the books we flipped through.
History does not care about them yet.
I wanted to tell the young man I was helping
that there were other ways.
But I didn't know other ways.
Guns are power; when you're young and poor
your body can be shaped up and sold off,
gambled for a shot at a better future.

So I helped him find books that glorify war.
He thanked me and I went back to my desk
to finish making paper dove ornaments
that would decorate a tree in the library
for an International Day of Peace celebration.
Under a dove's wing I wrote
please protect this boy.

Good Luck

A bird almost shat on me this morning. I watched it as I walked, convinced that the bird resting on a wire would be the seventh to get me. The last time I heard his voice: a voicemail, asking me to ride with him to DC for the protest against the Iraq War. By the time I said yes, it was too late. He was already up there. I went anyway, looked for him in the crowd and yelled with strangers at buildings and streets that weren't listening. I encounter dead birds a lot. Two years later, in Seattle, at another protest, there was one on the sidewalk with a cigarette near its beak. I took its picture and posted it in an online album entitled, "Dead Birds Don't Fly." Hummingbirds are attracted to the color blue; they scavenge for it in nature, clutch it in their beaks to weave into nests. People tell me it is good luck to have a bird shit on you. In the last email he sent me he wrote *9 fucking days to not die and I get to come home :) and I'm getting out when we get back, so Yea for ME!!!* I recently watched a documentary about resistance fighters in Iraq. A scene at sunset with a mosque in the background: so many birds flying around it. Bodies have been found with pulpy eyes because hummingbirds have pecked the irises out. I found a dead bird on my porch once, put it in a jar and kept it in my apartment until it began to smell. Walking home from that protest in Seattle, someone asked me what we were fighting for and I said *Freedom!* I wish I hadn't deleted those messages or his cousin's text saying he had died. Wish I hadn't thrown a beer bottle at the American Apparel window. In the documentary there were American soldiers running around and explosions in the distance. My beer bottle shattered but the window remained perfect.

Us Lost Boys

Somewhere now a postcard is in transit.
On one side, an island,
on the other just the word *thimble*.

We both have *bangarang* tattooed on our ribcages.
Most don't get it, but for those who do,
I say, *yeah, we can crow*.

On a rooftop drinking, he asked me *do you think I can fly?*
I said, *yes, if you've found
your happy thought*, unaware
what made him happiest was disappearing.

After the funeral I shot tequila
and spun around outside, trying to find
the *second star to the right* to carry me into morning.

We said we'd never forget. I can't
remember if we ever said goodbye.
I doubt we did because *goodbye means going away,
and going away means forgetting*.

If this is the story, I am the Wendy.
He is there, suspended in air and looking for adventure
as I ask from my chair *boy, why are you crying?*

I Am Not Afraid

Time goes and goes and I worry that I know less with each setting sun.
It is ok; this is just the story going the only way it could.
Listen, for a woman left lonely, I'd say I'm doing pretty well.
I used to race some druggie trying to get away.
The wind rushing our faces as we pushed forward.
Bird was some druggie. I was some druggie.
Were we racing each other or just ourselves?
So many times we snuck skunk-weed into concerts
and danced together like heathens around a fire,
knowing the whole world was about to burn
and we would be ash soon enough.
Last night I got stoned off year old weed I found in a shoebox.
Because the world is angry and I needed something
to take me away from faces
beneath sheets on Paris streets.
I know none of them are his face
but all those faces are his face, Bird,
even though your face is gone,
I see it with every bomb, every terrorist action.
So much anger, the world is stuffed with it,
full like me on Thanksgiving. Despite the sting, I am
thankful for everything. So cheers to the wind and confusion
and leaves falling so I'll slip next time it rains,
and here's to the pain of knowing that what once was
is gone forever.

More than Zero

As I waited to go home after the funeral I watched new recruits wait to be shipped off to basic. Young and excited, I wanted to say *don't*, but just finished my cigarette and flew away. The last time I saw Bird alive, his hair was gone and his muscles had grown. He picked me up and tossed me onto that hotel bed after I got too drunk to bike home. Every time I see a young man in an Army uniform, I think, for just a moment, that it's Bird. Before we fell asleep I asked how many Iraqis he'd killed. He just pulled me closer, which I think means more than zero. Leaving the hotel room the morning after, soldiers' eyes followed me down the hall. The next day an earthquake shook a crack into my apartment's wall, right above the window. Bird returned to the desert. I'd touch the crack, look out at the mountains, and wonder where he was. When it rained, water pooled on my windowsill. Our last night together we talked about how hair and nails keep growing once we die, which is a lie, our bodies just dry out. But I like the lie, it helps me imagine him asleep in the casket, looking somewhat like he used to.

Carry On, Carrion

I had my hands on him last night in a dream I forgot upon waking.
Some days are easy but when they're not I feel like drowning.

The clock has stopped in my mind
                        we are still wild manes and taut muscle, entwined.

          What is the use of being all racked up over a hunk of meat?

When I drive highways I count the corpses of animals.
The stains they leave behind on the asphalt are sometimes lovely
and it helps me forget the dead friends and lovers I've left behind.

It's not the animal's fault when they collide with cars
but we curse them and cry
not for the mess made but for the cost to clean it up.

It is the same when a drunk doesn't wake,
when a vein breaks, when a bullet
blows a hole through brains.

          I can still hear the sickening thump and tumble.

It has been years since I hit something on the road
and witnessed a thing left unbreathing and unrecognizable after impact.

It has been years since I held someone's stiffening hand in mine.

The clock has stopped in my mind
                        we are entwined, all of us floating and smiling.

Under the Sea

I once read a story about a mother explaining death to her young son. She told him that when people die they go to live at the bottom of the sea to make caramels. Bird died in a desert and was flown home to be buried. When bin Laden died he was buried at sea because no country would accept his body. I visit Bird's headstone to leave candles, cigarettes, and whiskey. In the mother's story, caramels float to the surface but the dead remain down there. I have visited Bird underwater in my dreams. We swim for hours. We've grown mermaid tails. I know it's a dream, but it feels so real I have sea-legs in the morning. Prayers were recited before bin Laden was tossed overboard. I've said no prayers for my friend, but I write him poems and worry that he'll hate them. It's beautiful down below, soundless so I can't hear what the dead are saying. Opening their mouths, only bubbles come out.

Día de Muertos, 2015

Dear Bird, it has been a long time
since I last saw you.
How are you these days?
I've returned from the Gulf of Mexico
and now that you're on my way to things
I'll try to be better about visiting.
That wind chime sure does sound nice.
Here, I brought some flowers,
let me clear a spot.
Your mom's been keeping up this plot nicely.
But that big flag is a bit much.
I never knew you had a thing for Snoopy.
Interesting how there is always something more
to learn about a person.
This fog rolling in is freaking me out a little;
it reminds me of *Night of the Living Dead*
and the dirt road and tall headstones
make me feel alone in a bad way.
If it weren't drizzling I'd light you a candle.
I'm sorry, but I forgot to bring the whiskey.
Next time, ok? Next time I'll remember.
There is no one to hear me scream.
I don't even shed a tear as I return to the car.

To Save, Press 9

The first time I realized Bird was gone I was swimming, just days after the funeral. If something goes wrong or the end of the world comes, I can dial up my voicemail and listen to those I care for say *hello... love you... miss you.* Or whatever it is their voices are always waiting to say.

We used to drive to the lake when it was hot and miserable and the only thing that could make us feel better was strong breeze, high speeds, and the cooling splash of water. Sometimes I think the sun killed him. My cell phone saves messages for forty days, so every few weeks I resave them. During a thunderstorm we were floating and looking at the sky when lightning struck a tree. Before that lake was a lake it was a farming community, small but prosperous. Now it's just submerged roads rotting away.

I deleted Bird's last message a month before he died. The first time he came back from Iraq he said *the sun shines so hard there it dries out everything, even me.* We were by a pool then. Without finishing his beer he dove in, can in hand, clothes still on.

I hope I die by water.

The Gulf Between

Sounds of funerals
are steel-strong threads
capable of bearing weight.

Amazing Grace, how
sweet the silence can be.

This is the gulf of memories; we are helpless
in the clutch of earth and water.

Struggling, the progress

   (if be there any)

must be measured in waves
or in dreadful glacier-like inches.

We're Wireless

I've sent Bird some emails since he died, thinking maybe those messages could reach him because like my laptop, he is not wired to anything. I have a cellphone with his number still in it though I know that number is no longer his number and that I will never call it. Deleting it would be giving up, letting go. I like to hold onto something long enough for it to hurt. Hug too hard, kiss until my lips are sore. In my dreams I walk the tracks from one run-down town to another. It's just my phone and me, out there between cities. In my dreams my phone never rings and I don't check voicemails. After Bird died I boarded a plane, promised the clouds this was the last time I'd plow through them. Walking downtown, I notice payphones are disappearing. Dial tones barely exist anymore. I never was good at keeping promises. Mid-flight I look out the window and wonder whose death made this possible.

Kelly Jones is a poet, educator, and baker who currently calls Greensboro, NC home. She has a BA in Literature and Social Justice from Antioch, an MFA in Poetry from the University of New Orleans, and is now working on a Masters in Library and Information Studies. In her spare time she runs *The Gambler Mag*, takes long walks with her dog, and drinks too much coffee. She is terribly fond of glitter, manatees, and Wild Turkey.

www.ingramcontent.com/pod-product-compliance
Lightning Source LLC
LaVergne TN
LVHW041313080426
835510LV00009B/970